By: Jobe Leonard

Copyright © Jobe Leonard 2014

This book is sold subject to the condition that it shall not, by way of trade or otherwise, be lent, resold, hired out, or otherwise circulated without the publisher's prior consent in any form of binding or cover other than that in which it is published and without a similar condition, being imposed on the subsequent publisher.

For information about special discounts, bulk purchases, or autographed editions please contact Jobe Leonard at
Jobe@LakeFun.com

Write to:

Lake Fun

1511 Mayflower Lane

Dandridge, TN 37725

Or visit:

www.LakeFun.com

Copyright © 2014 Jobe Leonard

All rights reserved.

Your Lake has a Lake Fun Book Available as well!

www.LakeFun.com

Always ask permission before going near the water.

Wear a life jacket while you are in or near the water.

www.LakeFun.com

Always have an adult watching while you swim.

If you do not know if an activity is safe, ask an adult.

Never swim all by yourself.

Swim only in designated swim areas.

Take a swim lesson before you go to the lake.

Do not swallow or drink lake water.

Swimming right after eating is not a good idea.

Never jump from a tree, bridge, or rock ledge.

Watch your step, the lake bottom can be dangerous.

Enter the water carefully to avoid unseen dangers.

If you wake up first, never go near the water.

Know your limits, do not go beyond them.

Never hold somebody underwater.

Never overload a boat, raft, or tube.

Do not try to breathe underwater using a balloon.

Never jump into the water head first.

Swimming during a thunderstorm is not allowed.

Take a break to rest after playing in the water.

Watch and be aware of others while you swim.

List your own rules for lake safety below.

1.

2.

3.

4.

5.

6.

7.

8.

9.

10.

www.LakeFun.com

(Sample ½ page advertisement only $149 per year)

Advertise with us!

Do you own a family oriented business or organization that makes your lake more fun?

Advertise in this **Lake Fun Book** for a low introductory cost of $149 for a half page or $199 for a full page for a full year.

Plus a FREE basic listing on www.LakeFun.com

For more information e-mail: Jobe@LakeFun.com TODAY!

About the Author

Jobe Leonard lives in Dandridge, TN. After attending Tennessee Technological University, he received his MBA at Lincoln Memorial University. He has over 20 titles published on travel, construction, and architecture. For more information on his current projects, visit www.Jobe.ws.

If you enjoyed reading this guide I would appreciate your honest review on Amazon, Facebook, or Twitter. Also tell a friend and help me spread the word. Send any questions to JobeLeonard@gmail.com

Printed in Great Britain
by Amazon